FIREFLY
RACING WITH THE
DOLPHINS

CHALAT RAJARAM

BALBOA.PRESS

A DIVISION OF HAY HOUSE

Balboa Press books may be ordered through booksellers or by contacting:

Balboa Press
A Division of Hay House
1663 Liberty Drive
Bloomington, IN 47403
www.balboapress.com
844-682-1282

Because of the dynamic nature of the Internet, any web addresses or links contained in this book may have changed since publication and may no longer be valid. The views expressed in this work are solely those of the author and do not necessarily reflect the views of the publisher, and the publisher hereby disclaims any responsibility for them.

The author of this book does not dispense medical advice or prescribe the use of any technique as a form of treatment for physical, emotional, or medical problems without the advice of a physician, either directly or indirectly. The intent of the author is only to offer information of a general nature to help you in your quest for emotional and spiritual well-being. In the event you use any of the information in this book for yourself, which is your constitutional right, the author and the publisher assume no responsibility for your actions.

Any people depicted in stock imagery provided by Getty Images are models, and such images are being used for illustrative purposes only. Certain stock imagery © Getty Images.

Print information available on the last page.

ISBN: 979-8-7652-4736-5 (sc)
ISBN: 979-8-7652-4737-2 (e)

Library of Congress Control Number: 2023922014

Balboa Press rev. date: 12/18/2023

CONTENTS

CHAPTER 1: THE SEARCH

CHAPTER 2: SEARCHING WITHIN

CHAPTER 3: THE SEARCH OUTSIDE

CHAPTER 4: PEACE AND HAPPINESS

CHAPTER 5: AMERICAN JOURNEYS

Chapter 1

THE SEARCH

A POEM FOR THE MIND

The mind that wonders, wanders.
Liking the stillness sometimes of the moment.
Racing at other times, and in dreams.
Dragging one's thoughts 'n emotions.

The pictures, music and posts,
Written and shared by so many minds.
Messages to ponder and respond to,
Recharging the state of mind.

So where in lies the truth? An Algorithm?
So many tools, lists and anecdotes.
To read, assimilate, let it go by...?
Mind games together then, as Lennon sang!!

Chalat Rajaram 06/02/2018

A POEM FOR TODAY

Moon through the foggy sky,
Like my clouded heart.
Mine not to question why,
Mine, to play my part.

Catholic funeral mass in Vietnamese,
Hindu prayer to ancestors.
All seeking inner peace,
Love for our brothers and sisters.

The sun is out now,
All the colors bright.
Bikers speeding, their fitted GoPro,
It's Sunday, it'll be alright!

Chalat Rajaram 03122017

AMERICAN CITIZEN

Born as an Indian,
Over two and forty years.
Now a Naturalized American,
Emotions mixed, as the time draws close.
Congratulations, you are o.k. sir.
As hundreds mill past the M.C.
The M.C. cracks jokes, the volunteers
Do their best, maintaining the peace.
I try to pass the time,
Think back at the past years.
Those glorious Indian Summers in my prime,
My present anxieties and fears.
Corporate America, greed, lies.
Hard work, loyalty, honesty, love.
Oath of Allegiance, family ties.
Beliefs, religion, the God above.
Thus, I sit and wait,
I ponder and listen.
As the Judge later, on this date,
Swears me in, an American citizen.

Chalat Rajaram 12151995

BRIGHT SUN

The bright sun or full moon,
Smell of fresh rain on the ground.
The traffic, the bad drivers.
The sounds I cannot share with you.
The neighbors walking dogs,
Trash day, they pull the cans.
The cold spell and dried up flowers.
The sound of crows, parrots, I cannot share with you.
The love you gave me,
Filling up my heart and soul.
The smile you left within me.
All these you share even more.

Chalat Rajaram 01212016

COVID-19

They said write 2020 not twenty,
When this year started anew.
A virus then lethal for over sixty,
Stealthy, started spreading in a few.

The pandemic so fast, first in China.
The world observed the devastation.
Soon Japan and then in Korea,
Denial still, the world, in many a nation.

People and leaders afraid to call the pandemic,
Politicians unprepared to contain.
In a few weeks, afraid to term pandemic,
Even as the world was reeling, in pain.

Morality, economy, the markets crash
Disease escalation, death, destruction.
Governments slowed, not a faster dash.
Mixed messages, panic, and agitation.

Nearing a million infected globally,
Thirty-five thousand dead on earth.
Death in health workers seen likely,
As PPEs scarcity highlights the dearth.

Mardi Gras and spring break crowd,
Weeks later the illness manifests.
Actions that later did no one proud,
The country was never seen at its best.

Now we need to hunker down further,
Pray deeply to give wisdom to leaders.
Stay home to help every him and her,
Deep emotions, anxiety, for feelers.

Three months later no end in sight,
No to testing yes for some, delay.
Just adding to disease, this plight.
Guessing game come what may.

Mixed messages still, guidelines changing.
Numbers not meaning a thing,
Talking heads, experts daily opining.
Where is the good news? What will it bring?

Spiritual sayings and new actions.
Planetary Gods and alignments.
Lighting oil lamps hoping for light.
Holy men in India, pleading to the elements.

Friendships nurtured; family separated.
Zooming, Skype, family calls bring hope.
WhatsApp messages many repeated,
Johns Hopkins shows the upward slope.

So, stay home on some days, lots to figure.
Wash the hands, clothes needing wipe down.
Sit and ponder, speak with sister, brother.
Stay positive, smile, and try not to frown.

Data changing daily, steps increase too.
As knowledge slowly is revealed,
Testing, treatments and what to do.
Guidelines for the surge that's expected.

So, calm the mind, with mindfulness.
Practicing prayer and spirituality.
In sleep, dreams, and wakefulness.
Share kind words to friends and family.

Another week left in April and yet,
Near forty-two thousand deaths.
Mixed messages, we continue to get
Close to a million positive tests.

Different studies, varying outcomes.
Double blinded small numbers,
Peer review unable so many times.
Anecdotal stories, of his and hers.

This pandemic has months to go,
Modern times unprepared like any.
Poems, podcasts, music, feeling low.
Hang in there, as we care for as many.

Prayers for the sick and who died,
Prayers for those not yet but will.
Prayers for the doctors, nurses who tried.
Prayers to get over this very steep hill.

Chalat Rajaram March 29, 2020, 8:56PM
Updated April 9, 2020, 3:40PM

COVID RAIN

Rainy all week, this Covid rain.
Washing over buildings, roads, and home.
We keep scrubbing hands, feel this pain,
Will the virus finding none, stop its roam?

Staying home, checking social media.
Religious events have come and gone.
Jokes, repeat posts, no new ideas!
Covid news from dusk till dawn.

Then came this poem with narration.
Of a village, trees, friends, an evening.
Of this traditional annual celebration,
The joy past years, that it would bring.

The sadness then, tugs at my heart.
Feeling suddenly what I had lost.
Not much I could do, for my part.
The rekindled memories hurt the most.

A few tears suddenly, a sense of peace.
Feeling detached, then acceptance.
Deep look within oneself, this not to miss.
Unconditional love, the inward glance.

Gather then oneself, to meditate.
Heartfully, to appreciate this love.
Know fully, also of destiny and fate.
Kindness from within, and from Above.

Chalat Rajaram 04152020 5:19PM

DEEP DEPRESSION

You return to grip me within,
I've felt this pain before.
No warning, one cannot win,
No way out of this closed door.

I know this too will end and leave,
It always does, the way it came.
Remnants of past, in a weave,
No way to give it form or name.

Set the healing already in motion,
Trust in the prayer, hope for deep sleep.
Wake up healed, a soothing lotion,
Plea within for mercy, if unable to weep.

Part of nature, of holding on.
Of deeds, past and present.
Of memories now, and ones gone.
Ego and thoughts make a deeper dent.

So, smile and go on, deserve it.
Ups and downs, roll with them.
Observe the lamp already lit,
Deep within, is your own shining gem.

Chalat Rajaram 06092020 1:30PM

DREAM CATCHER

A place for souls to meet,
Imagination, elaborate stories unfold.
The heart lights up the screen,
As the thoughts and mind roam.

Waking up mid dream to wonder,
Right back falling asleep sometimes.
Intermission and often picture lost,
Not knowing whatever comes next.

This illusion, this waking and dream.
Deep sleep when nothing experienced there.
Hide and seek, the shining heart remains still.
Always there, a reliable trusted companion.

Dreams then of a special meaning,
A foretelling, a future or past meeting.
Or passive thoughts, buried in psyche?
Churning out visions of memories.

Chalat Rajaram 07302020 4:45PM

FIREFLY

You come to me on a rainy night,
I've just turned off the electric light.
Now you sparkle so bright,
That I shut my eyes tight!

Firefly, Firefly,
Truly I wonder why,
In this world, full of grief.
You are so bright, and so brief.

I have many secrets to tell you only,
It is that I am so lonely.
That the dark night brings thoughts unholy,
That I might also commit some folly.

But I believe that I won't.
Know that though, you don't.
You are a pleasure for a moment.
My memory lane is for you to rent.

Firefly, firefly, whither thou gone?
Will thou also be reborn?
Or fade away before the dawn,
For me alone to await the morn?

Chalat Rajaram 070701980 written while staying at the room above the
clinic, at Anjarakandi, Kannur, Kerala, India.

GOLDEN SHINE AND OTHER SHORT POEMS

GOLDEN SHINE

The green leaves of the palm,
A resplendent golden shine.
My heart sees You in the calm,
This special moment is so divine.

ONAM

And on this Onam day I
See the same You, years past.
Felt and heard, far and nigh.
Too deep this maybe, a bit too vast.

BIRDIE

Hello little Birdie, you seem so young.
Beckoning me to this new path, why?
Soon your family, with high notes sung,
Bathed me momentarily in your ecstasy.

SHINE

what seems so bright,
On everyone! yes that's right,
Everything in your sight,
He and you, always that one light.

Chalat Rajaram 08172020 8AM
Revised 08302020 5:30PM
Added 9/12/2020 4PM
Added 9/27/2020 6:45PM

GRIEF FOR FIFTY, NOW OVER ONE HUNDRED THOUSAND DEAD

This country Ill prepared,
As a virus sneaked in unknown.
No name yet it's silent roam.
Weeks went by, the world,
Was shaken to its core.

Not any better in words or thought,
As the deaths, in their numbers
Soared as many weeks already passed.
Stay at home, without any testing,
Terrible planning, mistakes exposed.

Dependent on one nation for everything,
This country could not stand alone.
But alone it did, in numbers of
Those infected suffered and dead.
Yet, the mixed messages continued.

Those affected and suffering worst,
Still reeling some states, feeling it more.
A Nation in this most severe of pandemic,
As makeshift mortuaries, and bare
Funeral services for the dead.

Last goodbyes sometimes o'er texts,
Or hastily left note, no voice through.
An intubated lung with leaving breath,
This country, that always comes together.
Grieved all April, for over the fifty thousand dead.

Alas! no relief, one hundred thirty-eight thousand!
Deaths. Leaders and the many mixed messages.
Sending children to school, the preparation.
Politics in health care, questioning roles.
Grieve all July, for over hundred thousand dead.

Masks still not on, seems so confusing,
The people in different directions steered.
It seems like a show on the big screen,
An illusion not felt within, only just seen.
This has been the way, now so much worse.

And so, this must go on as Nature wills,
No sight of a rainbow over the hills.
Look within, do what's right, humane.
Seeing others as you, to lessen this pain.
Compassion, journey of grief, for our dead.

Chalat Rajaram 04252020 1530PM added last three stanzas 07152020
9:10AM
Modified 9/27/2023 4:44PM

GUIDING PRESENCE

Your guiding presence, your beautiful smile.
I catch my breath, remembering the style.
Your love has been unrelenting,
Amid the many questions, unbending.
The grief and tears, they continue.
For the family and me, you're still the glue.
Please keep coming to me with your love,
So tenderly, my beautiful dove.
Fill my heart with joy forever,
Help me open it more, channels wider.

Chalat Rajaram 03132016 6:45PM

HELLO

As in the early dew filled morn,
The birds greet the first sunlight.
Trees positioned to receive.
Glimpses of a golden hue.
Thus, you walk with me, Hello!
In the space between breath
And thought. If mind can be still
while walking. The bright yellow
sky in some areas, blue in others.
Sun shining suddenly on me.
Bathed in resplendence! Happy,
peaceful deep within, as you guide.
Everyone always, every day, even
when one is not aware; lost in
ego and thoughts. You remain forever.

CHALAT RAJARAM 11242020 7:06PM

ILLUMINATING ME

With this body, I felt and touched.
I heard, smelled, and tasted.
I ran, sped, slowed, walked.
I flew, rode, drove and braked.

With this mind I thought and learnt,
I cried, laughed, sometimes in anger, burst.
I dreamt, imagined, braved, and feared.
My ego control, new techniques gathered.

My soul I have oft been seeking.
The One had been waiting, prompting, shining.
My Consciousness, in depth, so knowing.
In death still alive, still illuminating!

Chalat Rajaram 10/28/19 11:18AM

LOVE, AND ALL THE REST

I have been loved and been in love.
Listen carefully now to the background music,
Love in the cooing words of the dove,
The glow, warmth in the deep lighted wick.

People, events, birth, and death,
Affects me the same as it does you.
When we discuss good and bad health,
Pour love and compassion in all we do.

Poetry and music moves me and you,
Mindful guidance and pleasure.
Friends sharing words old and new,
Of love and life, now and then to treasure.

Chalat Rajaram March 25, 2017, written at Las Vegas Nevada

LOVE IN THE SUN

The resplendent light,
The love so deep within.
Moving clouds shining bright,
Over oceans it has been.
Every morning same delight,
The love more felt than seen.

A walk then in the midday sun.
Cool breeze in the westerly,
Flowing from the wonderful ocean.
Thoughts straying, steady barely.
Staying in the mood so Spiritual,
Feelings that bless, no special ritual.

The sun has such power and orb,
The logos and layers in its system.
Unimaginable to feel the throb,
Planets, effects on us and each other.
We seek this beautiful light always,
Hoping never ending be the days!

Chalat Rajaram 04242020 7:20PM
Added 2,3 stanzas 05022020 12:35PM

MAGNOLIA TREE

You stood before me,
Three decades and more.
The swaying of your leaves,
In the wind and breeze.
Like my mind and thoughts,
The Light flickers when they sway,
Always shining though.
On you and in You,
When the leaves stop,
And become still, you
Teach me to be still.
Why do I see you differently now?

Chalat Rajaram 10172020 3:15PM

MAY MUSIC ENVELOPE ME

If music can bring back one to their youth,
The mind and agitation, it could soothe.
If only it could reach in, touch one's lonely heart,
Or perhaps, any other body part?

Why not then, explore more music?
Of different eras, genres, languages to pick.
Explore the within, though raw, still go in.
Find for oneself if healing, or hurt would win?

Isolation itself brings such depression.
Mood changes, following in quick succession.
Will music touching so deep, bring liberation?
An improvement in overall health manifestation?

So let one delve deep into this healing avenue.
Much to learn and practice, this knowledge new.
To make a difference, perhaps in most but a few.
Envelope with music, as nature does with morning dew.

Chalat Rajaram 03202016 on flight to OC from Houston

MY THOUGHTS

Thoughts take me to that gentle child,
Who soon will turn a man, self-styled.
To the jungles, deep and dangerous,
Where the lion cubs, around their mothers.

To the happy, carefree family.
The girls were so lovely, the boys gamely.
To the showbiz of the modern Olympics,
The sad state of today's politics.

To the freedom of the movement of birds,
The lulled joints of squatting cowherds.
To my own days as a tiny tot,
The little episodes, where I fought!

To the long stretches of green grass,
The wild cat, and the slow-moving tortoise.
My reservations, style, complexes, fun.
Dark roads, lonely nights, that had me on the run.

Thoughts that I do not comprehend,
Thoughts to write down, share and lend.

Chalat Rajaram 07101980

OCEAN CALLING

Sunny, late November
Day for an ocean drive.
Ocean calling, specially to
Undo face mask, face shield.
After morning rounds, PCH
A drive, loud classic rock.
Just few hundred yards away,
Guns N' Roses, ZZ Top,
Foo Fighters and Tom Petty.
Guitars whining now mixed with
The scream of a motorcycle.
Catalina hills, clear horizon.
Pleasure, peace, happiness
Warmth inside and out, blessed.
To share with neighbor and friend.
Families far and near, dear friends.
This late November day calling.

Chalat Rajaram 11282020 2:07PM

REFLECTION

The reflection of the light,
That I saw in the still of the night.
Sent me thinking.
I felt myself sinking.
Had I anything done?
Or something won?
Did vices add to my flaw,
Virtues within, but who saw?
Had I reflected the real me,
Just a burden to others be?
Was I living in vain,
Like mud washed away in the rain.
Did I really have persistence?
Or a monotonous existence.
I thought.
I sought.

Chalat Rajaram 01041975

REMEMBER THE TIME:
A CLINICAL ENCOUNTER

When I spent that evening I knew,
It was the last time I would
See you again. We both knew it.
I tried to tell you Goodbye,
I did not, but I should have.

You knew the time was close,
When you raised a hand to stop.
The music giving an excuse,
Your family will be here in a few minutes.

You knew. When you said so,
When you couldn't any longer get up,
That was your measure of the time.
You had done it, many times before.

The threshold choir cheered you.
Said, you remembered them;
Not afraid, just resigned as you asked,
Why your son would not sit more with you.

Then I heard of your death.
That weekend, long into the night.
Your son, he sat with you at the end.
Nourished your heart and soul as you left.

Chalat Rajaram 03172018 1:45PM
(On American Airlines 2251, Boston to Dallas)

THE DELIRIUM

Return from the amazing journey,
One that went back in time.
Fever, congestion feeling sickly,
Slipping into this delirium.

Vivid dreams not uncommon,
With two sisters and parents now.
My tears, dad's smile like the sun,
Mum with him, helping my low.

Out of control Mercedes in reverse,
With me in it, helpless!
Why no crash? this rhyming verse,
Still alive? It's your guess.

Remembering prayers in India,
To help the various souls.
They always help, being not so afar,
Still guide me in my goals.

Chalat Rajaram 9/13/17

THE DESERT CITY

The land, the monarchies reign,
The countries forming the Emirates.
Way of life, knowledge to gain.
Food, culture, desert and dates.

Skyscrapers, Burj Khalifa around Dubai,
Buildings of different shapes and height.
Clear blue, where the ocean meets the sky.
The sand, from where to take in the sight.

The desert large and sprawling,
Camels replaced by bike and car.
The dunes, endless and re-forming.
Playground now, from near and far.

Tent cities with own adventure,
Shows and rides, belly dancers.
Hookah lounges, moods to capture.
Local food, drinks and appetizers.

Leaving with memories made,
Shopping favorites and gold.
Keep remembering, let it not fade,
Let these stories be re-told.

Chalat Rajaram 1/11/18 at 12:20AM
Bangkok Suvarnabhumi Airport

THE EMPTY MIND

The pacing, relentless and fast.
Verbalizing, of memories past.
The crying, screaming, loud laughter.
Curses, of words no recollection later.
Mute, sometimes still; depressed.
Angry, the body and mind so agitated.
Dependent, sometimes less, failure to thrive.
Through loving care, the will to survive.
Seeing sometimes life going downhill,
The void for us and them, too big to fill.

Chalat Rajaram 06131997

THE KEYS

The blessings I have been given,
My life, family, friends, profession.
How do I comprehend all this?
The wondrous gift of writing bliss!

My mind to control, positive good thoughts.
To feel happy, thankful, be introspective.
Discard negatives, and there are lots.
Good intention, their power quite infective.

Let the strength within guide me,
In the everyday journeys.
Let me share, for all to see.
Of a fulfilled life, the secret keys.

Chalat Rajaram 07172014 4PM

THE MORNING SUN

The morning sun, bathes over me.
Lighting up my heart and spaces.
Gratitude, love for me to see.
As I meditate and say my graces.

Through the window the setting sun,
Fiery red, my heart still beating.
Twilight, then the day is done.
Night moon and stars, hoping.

In poets I've heard of the dark,
The journey we take half our lives.
Then know it as a calling, the hark.
The whales never afraid of the deep dives.

If half the day is darkness,
Then embrace and adopt that too.
The night, embrace its fullness,
Welcome it back yes please do.

Feelings in the heart, emotions.
Separation, and loss, grief.
The absence of one so special,
What more words can I tell?

Chalat Rajaram 04/08/2017 revised 5/21/17.

THE SAGA OF MITRAL STENOSIS

I start mostly with rheumatic fever,
The streptococcus being my master weaver.
Little children are my usual prey,
I soon settle in and plan to stay.
I swell their joints and cause all pain,
I hold on to their throats by my streptococcal strain.
I catch up with their hearts very soon,
If I don't, well that may be for them, a boon.
All this passes off very fast,
I've been getting ready for the full blast!
Soon reappearing, I'm so glad,
I laugh within, seeing them go mad.
The boy has now turned to be a man,
He soon got tired if he ran.
Steep climbs soon become a strain,
All part of the plan from my wily brain!
Heart sounds I make, for all to hear.
The stethoscope transmits them to the listener's ear.
I have heard sounds sometimes called murmur,
Exams are failed, for students that cannot hear.
Murmur, purr, they're all same to me!
Of what importance could they be?
Special jobs still in my plans, to do.
Atrial fibrillation, cardiac failure, to name just two.
The poor old chap gets worse, as days pass.
I don't let up, still running on full gas.

Doctors, nurses blame me for the fall from health,
Some, ultimately meet with their death.
Early nineteen seventy, this saga is different now,
Workup, treatments, follow up, mortality low.
Do pay attention all over the world,
Hope this saga changes and is not repeatedly told.

Chalat Rajaram 05061974

THE SUN SETTLES

The sun settles into the sky,
Golden rays shining through the cloud.
If this were a painting, would I buy?
I am usually not that bold.

The group then gathers in the room,
Poets, or those with poetry in mind.
Maybe a new poet, here would groom.
I remind myself to feel blessed, be kind.

I have to read what's been given,
A collection of poems to read.
To feel the mood or to liven,
In me to plant, many a seed.

Chalat Rajaram 1/10/19 5:23PM
(Illuminations, UCI)

THE TOUCH

Both apprehensive at first,
She gives an aromatic body massage.
Both having been through the worst,
Controlling sadness once so large.

Thai speaking with little English,
Age first, then Country, marriage.
Her husband's death, no one's wish.
For me, the turning back a page!

Both of us with losses, grief
Between expert kneading, advice.
Be strong, keep busy, do more.
Will I marry again? Roll the dice?

A widow trying to survive, earn.
For her son, herself, society's calls.
Relaxing muscles, keen to learn.
Fifty not a barrier, despite many falls.

So at Chiangmai, two souls meet.
An hour of honesty, respect.
The usual Thai way to greet,
Leaving later, nothing to expect.

Chalat Rajaram 1/9/18 4:29 PM at Duset Princess

TIME

As I sit now reading,
The clock's hands go turning.
It is a fact,
That I am guided in my track.
By this clock!
Who knows?
How many more turns,
There is to go before Destiny shows.
On me, growing moss, and ferns.
Time tells many a tale.
Time does not ever fail.

Chalat Rajaram 09061981

YELLOW BUTTERFLY

Waiting patiently today, you
Saw me long before I did.
When I finally saw the view,
Between the leaves where you hid.

Beautiful yellow, almost a ballerina.
Your face, was that a lock of hair?
Colors on you passing for a fashionista!
You sure knew today what to wear.

Mesmerized, I just sat watching.
Your feelers by now lengthened,
Your delicate feet, on cactus latching.
Neither in hurry, emotions heightened.

Thank you for beckoning me,
To glance at you from the roses.
To glorify you, store in memory.
Your pictures, now, are in many poses!

Chalat Rajaram 06012023 1:01PM

Chapter 2

SEARCHING WITHIN

A POEM FROM MY DREAM

Roses that give out the perfume,
Taste of the mangoes you consume.
Same in the light of the lamp,
Rain, its wetness and the damp.
Your love in thoughts and words,
The singing of the birds.
A poem from my dream,
Add to the combined cream.
The pain you feel and perceive,
The healing you all freely give.
It all is nothing but one and same,
It's where we go, from where we came.

Chalat Rajaram 8/5/2023 6:37AM
Added on 8/23/2023 10:37AM

AS THE SUN KISSES THE FLOWER

As the sun kisses the flower,
I let my thoughts hover.
Of the year going by,
What, when, how and why.

The people and friends matter,
During clear sky, and when clouds gather.
During typhoon or hurricane,
Much more, during the pouring rain.

The rain brings new life around,
Where birds, leaves, flowers abound.
Too much rain then landslides,
After the fires parch the hillsides.

Nature, happiness and sorrow.
Yet, who really wants to borrow?
It all goes together, happens side by side.
Face it my friend, there's no place to hide.

A third birthday without you dear.
To face life, and go forward without fear.
Such has been the way forever,
Birth, life and death and ties to sever.

Chalat Rajaram Started September 2017
Completed on 1/13/2018 4PM

BLESSING

A new dawn, a bright new day.
Prayers last night for family and friends.
Feel so blessed, waking today.
When will these COVID times end?

Then the roses burst from buds,
At the front and the backyard.
Bringing joy through the clouds,
Time to let go, drop my guard.

The times have not ended.
However, while a lot better here.
India now, life seems upended.
Yearning for health, calm the fear.

Death of the body, grief, sadness.
The soul never dies, never, they say.
Prayers, thoughts, faithfulness.
An effort to feel deep, to find a way.

Chalat Rajaram 4/8/2020 6:45AM
Added 2nd stanza 5/5/2020 7:15PM
Added 3rd stanza 5/6/2021 8:35PM
Added 4th stanza 6/12/2021 10:30AM

BRILLIANCE

The golden cloudless sky in the morning.
After the night of rain, lights up the
Tree, which seems adorned with Christmas lights.
Just one coniferous part, the rest eyeing the beauty.
The birds balancing on the highest branches,
For the sight and warmth; the glory
Of this Brilliant sun; this moment in
Time: the year draws to a close.
A year full of promise, of love, kindness.
A year still marked by the pandemic.
The Sun however is constant; ever present.
In the heart; illuminating this brilliance.

Chalat Rajaram 12/29/2021 8AM

CONSCIENCE

At the end of this year,
What consciousness has
Emerged, as ICUs observe,
Unconscious states in COVID
Patients on respirators.
Walking masked in a community.
Not much changed, as a second
Surge pandemic raging. You
Would not know, as the ego
Feels it's not mine or not me!
Knowledge, thoughts and
Memories differ.
And at other parts of the world,
This virus rampages on human
Bodies, behavior, and conscience.

Chalat Rajaram 12052020 6:30PM

DEEP FEELINGS AND MUSIC

How can melodious vocals so rendered,
Invoke deep feelings, tears, sorrow?
Is it the Soloist; is he or she so endowed?
The Divine within bringing out visions.

The crows have appeared more so,
They following me, or am I more aware?
In pairs or threes, they come or go.
My feelings then laid out so bare.

Rama compositions bring tears,
Visions of parents at Calicut.
Pry open the soul for thoughts 'n fears.
So much emotion, welling in the heart.

The artist denies his power,
Attributes it to the Divine.
He was the instrument, the giver.
Led me to the Place which was mine.

Chalat Rajaram
Over Arizona 6/16/16 11:23AM

DIVERSITY AND UNITY

Nihilism as part of centuries,
Masters of suspicion that we are.
Ego and the mind that rules,
Over lands, in space and time.

Come, togetherness fading.
With time and events, ego
Filled with falsities, Ruling.
Over masses, no oneness.

This was meant to happen.
Over centuries, experiments
With philosophies where mind
Ruled over oneness, unity.

Diversity, a catch phrase of the time.
Yet, that sets limitations, division.
Unity seems too farfetched, when.
Divisions and opposites matter most.

Chalat Rajaram 09122021 8:03AM

DREAM IN MIRACLES

When my friend tells me of
Her dreams, and her analysis
Of them, I relate and listen.
Not totally in understanding.

Then when I have dreams in sleep,
Sometimes bizarre, at other
Times, soft gentle and soothing.
I think deep, still do not understand.

The truth and what and why,
That I am affected deeply by.
Them, and the forms and twists,
Of the story unfolding again.

Earthly and ethereal, which is real?
Life, when they are so close yet
Separated now by only the thin veil.
As one can only truly understand it.

The miracle of consciousness,
That brings all, me to One.
Perseverance in the quest,
Churned constantly, receive the grace.

Chalat Rajaram 11072021 6:40PM

FACING DEATH

How does one face death?
Especially, during failing health.
When one is mostly alone,
Feeling desolate and forlorn.
When a disease like cancer,
Is eating one over and over.
When medications dull the senses,
The immune system is losing its defenses.
Reflecting on previous battles won,
As new pressures are brought on.
Anxiety, agitation, anger, and fear,
Grief, separation from ones very dear.
Emotions needing attention and care,
Kindness, comfort, hope to share.
Life nearing death, love, caring.
Spiritual connection, comfort, healing.

Chalat Rajaram 01191999

FOUR MONTHS LATER

As one looks back in time,
A construct only the mind has made.
Events, sorrow, death in the prime.
Why is the present allowed to fade?

Travel to India, the reunion.
Temple visits, leaving deep impressions.
Volunteering at a distant land done.
The deep cleansing, inward consciousness.

But back in time, go the thoughts.
Memories of the past four months.
No sense trying to connect the dots,
Let go defenses from all fronts.

Stay in the present, in love.
Be thankful, knowing we are but one.
Look within, not below or above.
A journey for the ages, until it is done.

Chalat Rajaram 09132022 9:29AM

FULLNESS IN EMPTINESS

The sun's gone behind the cloud,
The world now appears as a shroud.
The faraway clouds look red and proud.
Man, this scene I truly loved.
The speeding train carries me on,
I gaze at every bush and thorn.
The children whistle and blow the horn,
Somewhere, a soul is born.
Villages and towns, I pass.
As I smell the green grass.
I see the spread of water, bordering moss.
The goal, the soccer team experiencing loss.
Blackness now, spreading everywhere.
The pounding heart feeling bare.
Hillside silhouettes, where souls rest, spirits roam.
Thorny bushes grow, and tall trees form.
A woman's gentle moving pelvis.
As other trains, metal, and steel whizz.
And the dark clouds overhang,
Ready to open anytime with a bang!
A large patch suddenly of the Golden Sun,
Brilliance so special, akin to none.
I see Shiva and Vighneshwara,
The steps leading up to you, Om, Sri Ayyappa!
As now the sights change.
The trees seem to re-arrange.
The train charges on,
Onward, forward, it flies on!

Chalat Rajaram 04221980 6:40PM

GALAXY

Let me find the wind, all-powerful,
The one that churns the water.
Of heaven and Yang so masterful,
And water in yin, former or latter.

Let me experience dance,
Cowboy up or Cupid shuffle.
Feel the courage, take a chance.
Play the music loud, not a muffle.

And now read about the Trinidadian.
The words in the book to get lost in,
Ways of the mind, Jung or Freudian.
Come up for air or dive deeper, go all in.

Chalat Rajaram
April 21 2017 10PM

I CRY

I cry from loss,
I cry from love.
I cry from anger,
I cry from denial.
I cry, I cry.
I cry from hurt,
In me and others.
I cry from suffering,
I cry from knowing.
I cry, I cry.
I cry from deep within,
I feel the cry.
I cry just suddenly,
I cry a little, or a lot.
I cry, I cry.

Chalat Rajaram 05092022 6:31AM

LOSS

Did we not lose hundreds of thousands?
Nay, millions of bodies, to this pandemic
Across our vast globe, bodies of all,
Ages, caste, creed, color -
Bodies with ideas, thoughts, aspirations
Suffering, gone in a whiff!
Bad decisions, misinformation
Innocent or willful
Ill-prepared, naive
Ego-filled, selfish hearts
Where was empathy?
While millions of these souls left their bodies
On further journeys unknown.

Travel inwards to be better.
For others and ourselves
In countries across this globe.
Times call for a change in approach.
Early in life to care, find the Self, and
See others, ourselves differently, as one.

Chalat Rajaram 12/11/2021

PEEL THE PERSON UNDONE

I feel like writing a thousand words,
Of deep sorrow, or flight of birds.
My hopes, fears and aspirations,
Unspoken thoughts, the revelations.

Disease, chronicity and healing.
Of denial, guilt many a feeling.
Sorrow; deep and numbing,
Forcing one to go into hiding.

Of days and nights, the dreams.
The smiles, laughter, silent screams.
Shattered life, where's the sleep?
From here, nowhere to leap.

Poetic words and inspiration,
Friends and family, no separation.
Of kindness and compassion,
Peel the words, the person undone.

Chalat Rajaram 04042017

SPEAK TO ME SAID THE FLOWERS!

Speak to me said the flowers,
As the leaves brushed me.
The heavy branch caught me,
On my quiet detached walk.

Suddenly I noticed diversity,
Flowers, radiant in the sunlight.
Others bent on their stems,
Some dried up, many fallen.

Yet in their multitude one message,
Oneness, the joy of being the same.
As I probe into myself, without
Ego, thought or doer ship.

Neither enjoyer ship, special attachment.
No aversion, to feel we are the same.
Quietened the thought and mind,
As the flowers said, speak to me.

Chalat Rajaram 08132021 7:26AM modified on 09112022

THE CLIFF FACE

Been here for eons, this cliff face.
Witness to changes, too many to tell.
Time and space moving at own pace,
Steep drop tolls many a death knell.

The crashing waves on rocks below,
The foam and spray, moss, and algae.
Fauna and flora on the cliff come and go.
Humans sometimes just to write an elegy.

Hurricane and storm changed this cliff,
From sharp features to craggy rock.
The bending trees to trunks so stiff,
Nature knows nothing here to mock.

Night falls, freezing cold to starry nights.
Lovely sun and warm lazy days,
Comets seen at dizzying heights.
The cliff face hidden in cloudy haze.

In dreams and on journeys then,
The cliff face lends us a sight.
Illuminate memories, no need to pen,
Vision within, stories safe, alight.

CHALAT RAJARAM 07272020 12:19PM

THE DREAM, THEN A MIRACLE

On a rain swept and windy mountain,
No shelter, just run to your home.

The bitter cold and loneliness,
The lost way and many paths.

Home not far away, but where?
Then she calls to reassure.

Where are you? and your son?
He is not with me you say.

She understands, but still waits.
You are closer, now she's at the door.

As you rest in bed you know,
She brought you back and how.

Miracle even in the dream,
The vision, a blessing it would seem.

Four years later now, it seems real.
More time for the layers to peel.

Miracle, the self the real truth.
In all three states and the fourth.

Chalat Rajaram 11072021 6:20PM

THE DREAMS

Dream 1

The slowed traffic.
A gaggle of ducks behind,
A lamb with bloodied hind legs.
I parked my car near the gas station.
The lady also stopped, came across.
Are you going to help pay also?
Yes, she smiled putting her cards away.
As we both proceeded to the vet,
On Wynad Road, near my home.
She was bringing the lamb.
As my wife would have done.
SPCA came to my thoughts.

Dream 2

Telling this story to the DON,
The LVN is busy as always, on the phone.
My three sisters also there,
Do not ask me why!
I updated everyone about what the kind lady did.
Had heard from the vet. The
Lamb was doing well.
Also, the Armadillo, the armadillo?
Yes, she said. My thoughts now
Messed up, but then my wife passed me by.
As I continued with the story how much
All this ended up costing. The dream ended.
We would never know. SPCA should benefit.

Chalat Rajaram 04192020 6:33AM

THE MIRACLE

The tree appeared sad, for just a bit.
The leaf then asked, "What's wrong with you"?
The fruit knew something didn't fit,
The roots, they always knew what to do.

The birds on the branches felt comforted,
Generations had too, before them.
On the sweet ripe fruit, they nibbled.
Tweeting, chirping from branch to stem.

As his skin brushed past, touch remembered long ago.
The joy experienced, amidst buzzing of the bees.
The bushes, vines, also felt a deep glow.
Reflected deep, in their memories.

The mind, weaving threads of the story.
Changes, aging, as the leaves fall.
Happiness and the sense of Glory,
The Miracle, of the One in all.

Chalat Rajaram 12142021 12:52PM

THE VISIT

The nights and days, lived.
Looks, smiles, memories fade.

The drive over the bridge, the smell,
The setting sun, hearts that swell.

The sounds of Yanni at the Acropolis,
A birthday gift, good times that I miss.

The smiles, laughter and wit,
Special, somehow everything fit.

Now a presence, a dreamy vision.
A Blessing, life lessons, a mission.

What will happen, will always happen.
Journeys of moving on, remain then.

Chalat Rajaram 7:24 PM HK time September 10, 2017
Enroute to LA from recent Delhi visit

THIS PLACE I LIKE

This place I like,
Hey Mike!
With the smell of fresh cut wood,
And everything is so good.
Where butterflies haunt the bushes,
Everyone does what he or she wishes.
This place I like,
And of course, Mathew's bike!
This place, from where I can hike.
This place I do like.
The night owl's hoots,
The sounds of the dancing boots.
The spirit of my forefathers,
The smiles of the wood gatherers.
I like them all, Mike!
This place I like!!

Chalat Rajaram 02061980

TREES

Standing tall reaching higher.
As far as the eyes can gaze up,
Others grow sideways, stout.
Abundant leaves or scarce,
Branches galore or few to none.
Loving the sun, growing toward.
Finding different vantage for
Birds, and animals. To bask in
Moss amongst other co-dwellers.
Living in harmony, warmth, and shade.
Clouds sometimes reflecting trees,
Rain beating down, or snow and ice.
Cycle of life and death, of regeneration.
The seasons of change, the stillness.
The language of silence instilled lessons.
The deep consciousness, their own.
The trees that continue to speak and teach.

Chalat Rajaram 11202020 7:27PM

UNDERSTANDING

One that has not been understood,
For reasons, lost in the deepest wood.
Misunderstanding, many in the way.
Oft times, occupying the longest part of day.

The light shining through a spider's web,
The marks left, sand from receding ebb.
An understanding of quiet stillness,
The ocean and sky, this huge vastness.

Mistakes oft repeated, self not understood.
Been there forever, if only one would
Try looking in. A root deeper within to find.
Without the many thoughts in the mind.

The deep self! feel where thoughts arose.
Stay there, if possible, no need to sit pose.
Attention! caution! to heed is to know,
The flowing mind, thoughts come and go.

Even knowledgeable people have found it hard,
Emotions overwhelmed difficult to ward.
Oft repeated mistake, distance apart.
Many falls, then sorrow in the heart.

Detachment seems to be a first step.
Yearning for a teacher, seeking help.
This understanding happens very slow,
But peace with it, surely will follow.

Move forward with lessons and practice,
Remove the ego, mind, hers, his.
The squirrel, sparrow have fewer words,
Then heal within, feel free like the birds.

Incomplete 7/12/2020 complete 7/14/20
Chalat Rajaram 7/14/2020 8:07PM
9/27/2023 4:11PM

Chapter 3

THE SEARCH OUTSIDE

THESE DAYS

These days at the gym,
Sometimes going on a whim.

These days the aches and pains,
Worn cartilage, worse before the rain.

These days, where pleasure comes
From afar, smartphone, and hums.

These days where love feels deeper,
A smile, the joy then gets bigger.

These days and nights ever changing,
Cherishing. hanging in, hoping, longing.

Chalat Rajaram 6/13/17 7:45PM

REDISCOVERING MY VOICE, MY STORY

I feel the deep pain, a wounded healer;
Your stories here, couldn't have come sooner.
The sheer honesty, your giving nature;
Your help in guiding this story teller.

Be detached, message from my father;
In medicine, it helped me go farther.
Then this severe painful loss, this agony;
How do I now write, feeling this lonely?

Then redemption, these past few hours;
You helpful souls, vision of beautiful flowers!
Hope reborn, my journey can go forward;
End to this story, now feeling more empowered!

Chalat Rajaram
written at the AAHPM annual academy meeting Chicago
8/2/2016 9:37PM – breakout session "wounded healers"

OF FRIENDS AND LOVE

Their generosity, and loving kindness.
Fills you with awe, the oneness.
Not just you, their love flows for others.
Their many brothers, sisters, fathers and mothers.

A simple philosophy, their glory never sung.
Guided they are, truth now long sprung.
For they practice and follow this path,
Receiving as they give, of this no dearth.

Lessons to assimilate and wrap around,
The love that surrounds and abounds.
May I now gently slide into this way,
As I write of my love for friends this day!

Chalat Rajaram 10/7/16 1:45PM

THE VIOLIN

It had its days.
When it found its use.
Then touched with sanctity.
Any person handling it said so too.
A master once taught lessons.
Three pupils it had at the time.
Holiness attached to the instrument,
A world-renowned violinist used it once.
Now it lies in a corner,
Forgotten, its sanctity lost.
Uncared for, forgotten.
Life has moved on.
Broken, it lies useless.
Never to be touched again, it seems.
An article of rich culture,
An article of such heritage.

Chalat Rajaram undated 1974

THOUGHTS

Thoughts accompanied me in my walk,
It was my companion, with no one to talk to.
I seemed a stranger to all I met.
From them, only pitying looks did I get.
The thoughts were of the good old times.
Now gone, silent like the old bell's chimes.
Lovable thoughts, ones so heartening.
Happy thoughts, deep with their meaning.
Thoughts took me racing back to the past,
Leading me back to now, over all so fast.
I strained to forget them all,
It wasn't easy, took its toll.
I quickened my pace, no use!
It felt like the tightening of the noose.
Here, here, now it was all jumbling.
I felt everything within, exploding.
Relieved, as I was now nearing my place.
Exhausted as I took final steps to my home base.
No more thoughts, no, not again!
Not if I must remain myself, sane.

Chalat Rajaram 02021974

SLAUGHTERHOUSE

Brought in; tied both feet.
The animal looked far from neat.
A pull of the hind legs, he is down.
The onlookers give a small frown.
The neck is well stretched; and then,
A clean nick made by one of the men.
The animal bleeds mad,
A few of the onlookers look sad.
Soon, the last moments come.
As he dies, watched now only by some.
Soon dead, the poor chap.
The clotted blood forms a map.
All too soon, all so fast.
He would not be the last.
An animal lost for man's gain.
I'm hoping that it did not give him much pain.

Chalat Rajaram 03091975 written after the visit to the Madras
Slaughterhouse – preventive medicine tour of third year batch.

MY SPIRIT WITHIN

I grow within, thinking, contemplating.
My thoughts and opinions, express or rein in.
Knowledge, they say, is useless tinsel.
Without devotion, chime that bell.
Let my consciousness grow inward,
For me to see magnificence outward.
Oh Lord of this Universe, of all kin.
Help me as I stir my spirit within.

Chalat Rajaram 02242015 3:30PM

MEMORY BEARS REUNION

Memory of a touch, smell, smile.
Of personality, and varying style.

A special moment, an occasion,
A wedding, birth, or graduation.

A loving pet, a son, or daughter.
Sun's rays, or love of the water.

Of a war fought for a grateful nation,
Or goals achieved with true passion.

Of the stars, galaxy and the moon,
The good earth, a life taken so soon.

The role of this loving memory bear,
To bring love, in soul laid open, bare.

The compassion from the volunteers,
Coming from their hearts, fingers.

The feeling of awe the bears invoke,
No words for what they provoke.

The memory bears reunion today,
Share the stories, for healing I pray!

Chalat Rajaram MD 6/8/17 8:15PM
(memory bears stitched by volunteers with the clothes from patients who
have died)

RAGGING, A BAD DREAM

Three young girls were raped,
Forcing the removal of all they draped.
Scratching, clawing, and screaming,
They struggled, no one seemed to heed.
Some tried to save them,
The dignity, their inner gem.
But all in vain seemed measures these.
The scenes never seemed to cease.
It seemed like one gave way in the end,
In my mind, would she ever be able to mend?
As I watched, witnessed the scenes madly,
Ragging they said, as I turned away sadly.
Only to look at the unclothed freshmen guys,
Walking naked, per the seniors' ordering voice.
My nightmare was disturbed by the morning sun's beam.
Shuddering, as I woke up from the bad dream.
Today would be my first day at TDMC,
I knew it was not going to be easy.

Chalat Rajaram 01071974
(Ragging is the other term for hazing in the U.S.)

THE PROFESSIONALS

From my corner seat in the crawling bus, I see them pass.
The Professionals, flashing past in their fast cars.
8AM. Yeah, that's their time to start the engines.
The mission, the same every day, no one wins.
They pass almost in unison, as if in a line.
I look out each time I hear an engine whine.
Some burly men in small cars, smaller men in bigger ones.
A few are women of course, hair so neatly done.
Some travel in carpools, some look rather grim.
But most of the professionals look very prim.
These are men with destiny, calm and relaxed.
With reputation in the different fields. Specialized.
I got off the bus, it could well be pulled by snails.
I trudge on, my mind thinking still of these tales.
I reach the side gate, see the cars now neatly parked.
All the different lovely colors so well marked.
I smile within, another student following dreams,
Learning closely the art, science, what it means.
Thus, from the corner seat every day, I see them pass.
The professionals, flashing past in their fast cars.

Chalat Rajaram 07131975
(as a medical student riding a bus, watching lecturers, professors drive)

RING - RING

He slips onto her finger the wedding ring,
With hopes of what the marriage would bring.

The young man lazily blows out a smoke ring,
His mind is never dull, always imagining!

The pelvic bones do form a ring,
The newborn through this swing.

The schoolboy also awaits a ring,
For school to end, joy it would bring.

So many thoughts in my head from the word,
If only I could sing and be free as a bird!

Chalat Rajaram 07091980

NEGATION

Negation has struck again,
Forebodings of disaster looms.
I fight what could be illusions,
Feeling guilt stricken, I ask
Man, do you care? What remedy
Do you have this time, hypocrite?
As waves keep hurling at me,
I want to run, hide, and fight.
Stand up and fight.
Don't run, the path is showing.
Wait, let the senses rise.
There is reason to prevail.
Let the devil go.
He would be lurking in other corners,
He would find others to sow grief.
He would other poets.

Chalat Rajaram 10251983

LIFE

Knowing not what to write,
I try, try as I might.
To see Life, to know it.
And to love it if I am but fit.
I knew her before, well a little bit.
She was then with me every bit.
I loved her, as she had loved me.
Now without her, I'm like a lonely bee.
Every inch of her, I enjoyed.
To move with her, I was overjoyed.
She was never without me.
Ever together, yes, whenever be.
Now often, I think why she left me,
Leaving me feeling rotten, as you all can see.
I pray, and pray, she comes back soon,
It is, you know, soon to be June!

Chalat Rajaram 05101974
On the eve of Pharmacology results, to ensure myself to enjoy life in June.

PANTOUM

When I read the different posts,
The different posts, when I read.
The striking variety stretching,
I read, when the different posts.

The deep meaning, then why questions?
The questions, give answers, deep meaning.
Their different origins, these questions,
Meaning then, answering the questions.

Are they questions? or the deep meaning.
Posed by the folks on the WhatsApp?
The questions could be the meaning,
Their answers, as I read the different posts...

Attempt at Pantoum style of poetry
Chalat Rajaram 0312201810:50PM

"ELEPHANTS" A PASSION

This unique experience at Chiang Mai,
A difficult drive up the mountain.
Mine now not to question why?
Compassion, more knowledge to gain.

The elephants are gentle though big.
Young and old they exude love,
Rolling around in the dirt they dig,
The babies always get the wow.

So, we hiked up many high hills.
Narrow bridges and cut out paths.
Playing with the mammals our hearts fill,
In the river with them, joining in their bath.

The mud spraying and rubbing.
The glee and mirth of these giants!
The playfulness, active listening,
Their trunks are like water hydrants!

Memories of the adult and baby,
Of a place the ecology a priority.
The fruits and joy for all to see.
So far away from their captor city.

Rescuers were special folks. A passion
To free them back into the Wild.
Captive then, chained to their den.
Their faces now, like they have smiled.

How lucky then in this lifetime,
To witness such passion, to marvel.
Freed elephants in their prime,
Their stories are for me to tell.

Chalat Rajaram
At the Elephant Jungle Sanctuary
1/9/18 at 5PM

LIFE ACROSS THE SKY

There must be discomfort and pain,
Feeling hopeless, someone with nothing to gain.

Pain physical, emotional and spiritual.
Expressed outward, or the look so visual.

Pain of suffering existence, of terminal illness.
Ignored often, strewn in between words of wellness.

Looking back at our own past experiences, teach us why.
As I ponder questions of life, across the sky!

Chalat Rajaram 02242015 3PM

EIGHT MONTHS AND FATE

Wandering around the Titanic exhibit
On 14th April 21st August you both were hit.
Fate had been sealed, yet no one knew.
Now alone, mourning with the gathered few.

Nightmare last night, a pool bloodied.
A beautiful dog, shot, floating, now dead.
Thoughts go back to you, eight months, and fate.
Wondering my turn, coming through the gate.

Chalat Rajaram 04172016 8:45AM

I WAS.

I am a bird in flight,
Having flown many a day and night.
I could never stay too long,
Wanted ever to belong.
Flapping my wings very early,
Leaving my home frequently.
I have never known anything lasting,
As I've viewed events only in passing.
I then met another bird so dear,
I thought in my head to marry her.
She then flew back, her own way.
I was resigned to facing what then may.
Now I fly in despair round and round,
As the dark clouds abound.
Wanting to finally see a break,
From this bad dream to be awake.

Chalat Rajaram 07041973

AFTER THE RAIN

It was after the rain,
That a man was in pain.
Whence I was called,
By another, not entirely bald.
The jeep took us to a place remote,
The birds were loud, rendering their notes.
I walked uphill and down,
In the mud, wet and brown.
Through narrow paths, between rice fields.
Feeling the bright-eyed stares and laughing kids.
My rubber shoes squeaking with water,
Walking by the river, as I suddenly saw her.
The young pretty woman, with breasts held high.
She stopped, staring as I passed by.
I walked over the hill, under shady trees.
Hearing cattle moo and singing bees.
Until I finally reached the man in pain,
It was just after the rain!!

Chalat Rajaram 07071980 – after making a home visit at Anjarakandi, near
Kannur, Kerala, India.

FREEDOM

I yearned for the freedom of driving,
The day was both exciting and depressing.
The traffic then slowed, snaking, weaving.
Turning around, I started retreating.
Changing radio stations, the schoolteacher,
Telling the story of her dead husband.
Then there was the mad preacher,
Awaiting the word of God for his band.
My thoughts went to patients, physicians.
Contracts, bonuses, layoffs, operations.
Sorrow, happiness, health, illness.
Wife, son, exercise, Singapore Airlines.
Suddenly, the open road, freedom!
From the clutches of these thoughts.
The music more pleasing, I start to hum,
As the rain comes down in drops and lots!

Chalat Rajaram 03041993

Chapter 4

PEACE AND HAPPINESS

857575 STEPS

Getting closer to a million steps,
Over seven months, each one helps.
In getting out, observing nature, life.
In happiness, sadness, during strife.

Mindfulness, prayers, meditation.
Blessings of this creation.
Churning the truth every day,
Love and peace flow this way.

Many births, deaths, and graduations,
Weddings, engagements, separations.
Health issues, investigations, medications.
Anxiety, spirituality, determination.

Each step revealing a message,
Guiding towards well-trodden passage.
Losing ego, building on happiness,
Exercising daily on wellness.

Mindfulness, search for God within.
Detachment, understanding, Zen.
Steps for physical, emotional healing.
Self-care, self-understanding, well-being.

Chalat Rajaram 07212023

BRAHMAN

Awareness and just that,
The bird in front, frolicking.
Both bird's, and my mind, thought
Mix as one, now we are enjoying.

The one consciousness, peace.
All else just an illusion,
The selfies, the diving, tease!
Remove it all, completely undone.

A dream, delusion, body, ego
Real and unreal, changing.
Always, many forms and more,
Detach from all just once, stillness existing.

Brahman, always the one truth.
In the bird, me, all, and you.
The suffering, illusion, to soothe;
Ever shining everywhere, never once new.

Chalat Rajaram 02042023 6:14PM

GARLAND

Walking along the ocean,
Feeling the wet soft sand.
Shining on waves, the bright sun,
Whence I came upon the garland.

There they lay, many strewn.
Across the beach, every size, shape.
At evening time, day, and noon.
Sometimes drawn back in, by a wave.

On the waves, the sun reflects brightly.
Feeling within my consciousness.
The same light everywhere, so surely.
Sharing in the same one happiness.

Stories from deep within the water,
Resting amongst kelp, urchin, sea star.
Abalone, jelly, mussel, they all matter.
Creatures of ocean, from near and far.

Swimming with and through life forms,
Man, his selfish motives, hurting.
Nature trying to maintain its norms,
Weather changes, oceans deteriorating.

Fires, hurricanes, and tornadoes,
Storms, floods, many landslides.
Our part not recognized in many woes,
As the different systems collide.

May our combined common sense prevail,
Enjoy many more garlands to decorate.
For generations after, let's not fail.
Let love grow everywhere, lose the hate.

Chalat Rajaram 08232023 8:18AM

GOLDEN LIGHT

The howling Santa Ana winds,
The wild swaying of many a tall tree.
Golden color of leaves through the blinds,
Shining as brightly within, happy, free.

Amidst the thrashing of branch, tree.
The mind and thoughts run wild,
The rays of the sun shine steady,
Show the way, calm the mind like a guide.

The golden light within, shining
At all times, from birth to death, beyond.
In deep sleep, in waking and dreaming,
Do go back in, envision a stronger bond.

The mystery of this life, meaning.
The same for them, you and me.
The deep trust to keep forming,
The golden light shining so brightly.

Chalat Rajaram 01262023 7:35AM

HOST OF BOTTLED DAFFODIL

Amongst diagnostic aids,
And trolleys, neatly made.
The case notes files,
And ECG, running miles.
Amongst the many nurses,
The oft-changing physicians.
The room so noisy most times,
The rare silence sometimes.
Looking on, at smiles and fears.
And at laughter, many tears.
With only a little room to fill,
Stands a host of bottled daffodils.

Chalat Rajaram 04031983
Birmingham Accident Hospital ED department

MAKE AMERICA HEAL AGAIN

This new acronym MAHA,
In my heart, I feel the word heal.
One does not need to go far,
There are no layers to peel.

Just reach out, or just be there.
Keeping still and observing,
Detach, remove this ego here.
Grief has stages, and we are experiencing.

This Nation has been dealt severely,
A pandemic, this unrest to boot.
Pick ourselves up, lovingly.
Yes Love, go to your very root.

These are trials America must face,
No escape, we need to trust
In ourselves first, then keep pace.
Avoiding negatives, our healing is a must.

Pray in our hearts, to God or not.
Take hold of yourself and heal.
This moment will mean such a lot,
For life, the giant turning of this wheel.

Chalat Rajaram 05312020 6:45AM

MAUI FIRE

Maui, the gem of Hawaii.
America is now grieving, reeling.
The visions, hard for you and me.
Such a great loss, so devastating.

Fire and the severe destruction,
In death and dying, journeys varied.
Recovery and grief, bewilderment,
Every spiritual healing, from the seed.

Chalat Rajaram 08152023 5:45AM

MEMORIES OF WIND

Getting out this morning,
The sun, warm and benevolent.
The Santa Ana's kicking up,
Swirls, and full-on pressure.
The camera, picking up
Motion of the trees, swaying.
Birds chattering in the branches.
A few are caught up on irregular flights,
Some sit on rooftops, just sunbathing.
Memories of walks long ago, on such days,
Wind swept amongst paddy fields.
The wind chimes speaking,
The same words of the mighty wind.
Memories of temple bells in a
Faraway land, same awareness always.
A small insect crossing the road,
Feeling windy vibrations on the cement below.
The warmth, the wind, the One.

Chalat Rajaram 03072022 10:17AM

MORNING AT THE BEACH

Pigeons at the beach,
Glistening green and pink.
Sun shining on their necks
The iridescent colors show.
The little bird on a rock nearby,
Alone, and enjoying the
Waves, the rising morning sun.
Playing with the spray thrown up,
Flying up and straight down.
The seagulls chilling on the sand,
A lone gull resting alone, further down.
Stands up at my approach,
Anxious look, then I see her baby.
Running in the water, picking up
Nutrients washing ashore; mum.
Wanting to rest, tired with her many
Mothering duties! Till I showed up.
Inquisitive of her life, and the baby gull.
Protective, approaching me, a step.
Or two, with one eye on her child.
Life, this morning, in the ocean.
These myriad activities, in my mind.
Stillness constant, activities apparent.
Ocean, the Sun reminding of the One.

Chalat Rajaram 02082022 10:53AM

MOTHER TO ALL

The temple at Attukal,
Such energy and vibration.
Its own to feel, experience.
Large crowds, this Sunday morn.

Tall Brass lamps, multiple
Wicks, oil, and thread on lime.
That has been turned inside,
Out. Sitting neatly in carved areas.

Multiple tiers, on the large, tall lamps.
Beautiful sight to behold, the light.
I walk in with offerings to Mother.
Devi, Bhagavathy, my gaze on her.

I feel her stare too when I walk in.
I carry a garland of green limes.
Snaking lines of devotees, pushing
Bodies one against another.

Usual sights at famous temples.
While I walk forward, on the wrong
Side, with no one there. Until a
Security man stops me, to turn around!

"Join the snaking line", he said.
Two women I had not seen, now there,
The one next to me said, "let the old man in;
Let him join the line here".

Security man said no, I had to go back.
He turned, went the opposite way.
The lady beckoned me to go under the dividing rope,
Let the second one too, I thought they were together.

The line allowed us to join, no complaint.
I turned now, thanked the woman who helped.
With a broad grin she said so sweetly,
Am I not Mother to all? Then disappeared.

Chalat Rajaram 05312022 2:51AM modified on 09112022

NEEDLE

The energy is running wild.
In the tissues of this body,
Degeneration aided by
The mind and thoughts.
Affecting the senses.
Causing Pain and suffering.
Just as breath control,
Pranayama, tapping into
Energy flow heals by
Harnessing the mind.
The needles placed.
In the various paths,
By the acupuncturist,
Change the patterns and
The pathways aided in some.
By Knowledge of the Self.
Magic of healing multi-pronged.
Physical, cognitive, emotional,
Existential, spiritual.
Inner Truth guiding seeker,
To The healer, the needle.

Chalat Rajaram 11112022 4:05PM

NO THOUGHTS – MY REVERIE

In my walks and between thoughts,
The gentle running steps, little tots.

The singing of the birds everywhere,
Joyful hearts theirs', always anywhere.

The orchid bursting again from bud,
The gladiolus rising in the potted mud.

Roses and bees, gently taking their lick.
Portioned, no greed, as they dart and pick.

Thoughtless, absorbing it all in,
The oneness, without and within.

This joy and peace, all in a big gulp,
As thoughts arise again, breaking it all up.

Chalat Rajaram 04192022 1:05PM

CHALAT RAJARAM

OUR JOURNEY

I have been on an unlearning spree,
The knowledge is out there for free.
Staring openly, like all parts of the tree.
Buried in a single seed, the result for all to see.

Why then these divisions? desire to be free.
The self in one and in all, this racial diversity?
The body, ego, mind, all that control me,
The thoughts, leading everyone separately.

Life matters in every story.
When everyone should address equity.
The bright light within to guide you and me,
Honesty and courage, in our everyday journey.

Chalat Rajaram 02152020

POETRY AND PAIN MANAGEMENT

Can poetry really kill the pain?
What then really can I gain?
Deep feelings I need to write down,
So, I may gently remove your frown.

I love this idea to write a poem,
Seated, on top of that large dome.
Feeling the wind against my ear,
The radiant warmth, feel without fear.

So, I hope to ease my pain and yours.
Know that there are no rules or laws.
Just you and me, to relax and trust.
The healing comes, like magic dust!

Chalat Rajaram March 11, 2016
AAHPM meeting Chicago

CHALAT RAJARAM

RACING WITH THE DOLPHINS

You fell. It took forever.
Your life now behind, a new journey.
You wrapped your love, it felt so dear.
You let go gently. We let it be.
Your leaving, spiritual and so sublime.
Held your head high, what courage!
You left listening to favorite hymns,
You completed your final page.
You helped guide the ceremony.
Eloquent recitals of Sanskrit words.
You controlled the elements, kept it sunny.
As you soared, high like the birds.
You were happy, joyful.
Showing your childish mirth.
You gently tread water, not fearful.
Racing with the dolphins to the depth.
Then you rose to the skies,
Your frame looked beautiful.
You smiled at our goodbyes.
The sun's rays on you were bountiful!
The clouds soon parted,
As Aditya shined brighter!
You were free, as ocean and sky joined.
Vaikuntam awaits Dad, rise higher!

Chalat Rajaram 03182006

SILENCE AND GROWTH

May the silence help the growth,
Quit the mind, thought or both.

May there be no strong attachment,
Feeling no aversion, but sense of detachment.

May I exercise caution, revisit a feeling.
Give pause, let love lead my dealing.

May this exercise continue night and day,
The silence and growth, dance within and play!

Chalat Rajaram 04302022 7:41AM

SLOW LEARNER

A slow learner of life.
In life, about life.
About the purpose,
Ego, thoughts in this life.
About mind and wandering,
In this and other lives.
A slow learner of books,
Of crafts and tools, of nature.
Of the meaning of life.
Of births and deaths,
Of the One undying Self.
Of caution and controls,
Of love, attachment, a
Slow learner of detachment.
It has always been like this.
Awareness, the slow grind.
This truth of the slow learning.
Relief and release that,
This is nature, the way it is.
It has always been this way.
Just stay in it, thou art that.

Chalat Rajaram 03082022 3:36PM

SPIRITUALITY

Spirit actualization, Spirituality.
Exploring, with a caring mentality.
Trust building, sharing honesty.
Walking together, this life journey.

A pause, a glance, silence.
A tool, gently breaking defense.
This then, a lifelong practice.
Within, with all, hers and his.

Chalat Rajaram 07232022 7:02AM

SPRING SING

Beautiful kids singing at the chapel,
The joy in their hearts, blending so well.
We were invited to their spring sing,
And feel the happiness they bring!

They sang praises of the Lord,
Little voices reminding us of God.
Let us all rejoice this special day,
Success for all this school's kids, pray.

Chalat Rajaram 05031998

STIRRING, MAJESTIC GLIDE

A few days passed, then a stir.
The white birds have left a void.
From the neighbor, a picture share,
The heron standing atop the hood.

Not a stork, but instead the heron.
At my garden, smelling a rose.
My still posture now, gaze drawn.
The leaves stirring, watching close.

Then, the sudden surge, flapping
White wings, where leaves stirred.
The lovely large heron gliding
Towards me, my smile deepened.

The blessing, this is nothing else.
Deep faith, plea, love unfolding.
Chime all the multi-sized bells,
This is ecstasy fully blooming!

Chalat Rajaram 10202022 7:34PM

STORKS AND MAGNOLIA TREE

You stood before me,
Three decades or more.
Now, cut and removed, empty.
The space, like heaven's floor.

The swaying of your leaves,
Were like my thoughts and mind.
In the wind and cool breeze,
Ego filled, yearning to be kind.

Light flickered when branches swayed,
Though always shining brightly through.
At night, and day, shadows played.
The space still shines, the heart always knew.

The healing white storks visit every day,
Gazing at the space and me.
The leaves no more, the sky now gray.
Whiteness, stillness, to feel, see.

Chalat Rajaram 10092022 8:48AM

THE BIRD OF HAPPINESS

You appear during meditation,
In my deep concentration, at the Sun.
The rays spread through to
Strengthen the body and mind.
A glass door separates you,
As you hop closer and closer.
Little brown soft feathers,
A brilliant chest of red.
Beautiful curious eyes that
Look into mine, nervous, bright.
You turn to face the sun.
For a few moments we share,
The same rays, the same vision.
The same consciousness, it seems.
My one-legged hand folded pose,
You on your dainty tiny feet.
The mystic bird of happiness.

Chalat Rajaram 01242022 5:07PM

THE CROWS

They fly in flocks, these crows.
Every day without fail.
On rainy, sunny, windy days,
Their numbers and flight paths differ.
Like my wandering mind and thoughts,
They alight on branches, suddenly leave.
Just as the branches themselves sway,
For no unknown reason, except.
Wind outside and in me, the breath.
They watch me meditate, as I observe them.
Sitting on the highest branches, feeling
The warmth, the light, the peace from the Sun.
I feel the brightness within me shine,
And know they too share in the One.
Days, months, and years pass.
New generations of crows fly this path,
Where only consciousness remains.

Chalat Rajaram 02142023 9:17AM

THE MIRROR

Do always trust the mirror,
It shows you the way you are.
It needs cleaning to reflect better,
The bigger it is, one able to see far.

Look within, and the screen is bright.
Keep it clean, even better clarity.
When all is quiet, or not, always the light.
To see oneself, deeply, and happy.

The one in waking, dream and sleep;
The one ever present and shining.
Why then do we still suffer, weep?
Not trust in this bright glowing.

The mirror that poets have used,
To describe Consciousness within.
The truth we have oft missed,
While led in ways we did not mean.

Chalat Rajaram 01212023 6:15AM
Added on 03192023 6:35PM

THE NEST

The time of the year,
When birds of different kinds,
Different colors, sizes,
Pick up materials for
Nest building, rearing.
The young ones from
Past two years, have grown,
Become independent.
Yet one sees some dependence.
As humans procure homes,
Building or changing their own.
Older parents saw their children
Coming back. Fear. Anxiety,
Covid has now lessened.
As we build larger nests demolishing older.
The birds keep pulling at dry branches,
Which would not let go of mother tree.
Nature allows so much around us.

Chalat Rajaram 03102022 8:52AM

THE OCEAN

The sound of the waves at night,
A booming rhythm, that feels right.
The water, diverse, gains its might.
The dark night, elusive of sight.

Memories of a boy, figures in sand.
Writing names using his hand.
The sea waters, felt like a magic wand,
Clearing names, gravel off the land.

The memories their impermanence,
Thought in the mind, weave a dance.
Rising, falling, limited short stance,
Short span of flower, it's fragrance.

The thundering waves rise and fall,
The ocean's truth, all night, hear the call.
The journey within, feeling now a lull.
The Oneness, pointing to the Real,

Chalat Rajaram 02052022 8:25PM

THE SUN

Millions of rays emanate.
From You, shining light, and
Giving warmth to sentient,
And non-sentient beings.
Everywhere, in this wide world.
In forests, mountains, caves.
On and under water, creatures
Seek You every day of their lives.
You do not discriminate from good,
Or bad, powerful, or weak, from pretty
Or ugly; from large or small.
Your reflected Consciousness
Mimics our Own, to replenish.
We fail to understand, to stay within.
Thoughts and ego veil the truth, every time.
You shine always, through it all.
This illusion continues in waking, dreams, and in deep sleep.
You show the way, you remain. The One, constant.

Chalat Rajaram 01202022 7:55AM

THIS BIRTHDAY

This day means much more,
A pandemic year so many lives lost.
We still work, your hearts still pour.
Praying that we've seen the worst.

I am lucky to be here with you,
Not taking any of this for granted.
Hoping still to contribute, to do.
My calling, as yours too, was destined.

Feel this blessing sharing this day.
Keeping our hearts in this together.
Enjoy this special birthday in May,
This year will be like no other.

Be it spiritual, in words or art.
In dance, music, all from the heart.
This batch has grown, in many ways,
May this be for years, months, days.

Flowers, new buds, ever renewing.
The birds they know, ever sensing.
Our bodies too, the ever present I
Year to year we go, not asking why.

Chalat Rajaram 05162020 11:15AM

TURQUOISE

If a color was a notion,
A look and associated motion.

If a patient and illness,
A daughter, and her mildness.

A nurse and her compassion,
Her hard work, the dedication.

If these were oneness in consciousness,
Then seeing them separate, ignorance.

Chalat Rajaram 03272023 6:53PM

WATCHING THE EVENING

The large red sun going down,
Further bright, the red stones of the fort shine.
The milling crowd, dark, fair, brown.
On the many homeward buses, they pile.
An awesome sight, a near stampede.
Look out boy! That was close.
The shouts that none seemed to heed.
Cornered, some folks froze.
The railway station, not far away.
Panic scenes with crowds here.
Dirt and water splash on the unwary,
Horse carriages seem everywhere.
The evening lengthens,
The mood is changing.
Furrows unwrinkled, peacefulness.
Faraway music, now blending.
Alighting from the bus, I walk on.
Taking in the sights and sounds.
It's night now, memories not gone.
I write, put all the words down.
A blessing to feel and ponder,
Watching the evening here.
An experience to share and wonder,
My love for all to hold so dear.

Chalat Rajaram 09011983
Recalling an evening in Old Delhi
Poem written while in London, England.

WHAT THE OCEAN REVEALS

Knowledge of the Self, many stops.
Thoughts in the mind, this ego sense.
The storm begins as rain drops.
Explanation impossible, experience awareness.

Removing the thoughts, ego, mind.
Notion of waves, ripples, unaware is the ocean.
Rising always, as seen by the wind.
No explanation, exercise your caution.

Life experiences, good and bad.
Calmness, riptide, waves are still water.
From this ego, happy and sad.
The ocean reveals much, oneness does matter.

Chalat Rajaram 03042023 5:40PM

WHEN JESUS CAME DOWN

Amidst the cold benches, the pew.
The dim lights within and
The brightness outside.
The candles, the flowers and
The fragrances in the Chapel.
The soulful Mariachi,
And the deep, touching,
Hymns sung by the
Priest. The announcement,
Followed by raising of his arms,
Far above his head. That is when,
Jesus came down.
Into every heart at the same moment.
Sharing the One with another.
Spanish, English, Sanskrit,
All just one language of love.
The love that emanated was the
Love already within. The Love
Jesus, Allah, Krishna, Rama
Proclaimed. Love does not
Change. Bodies do.

Chalat Rajaram 02262022 6:50AM

WHILE ONE WITHERS

The first bud, then flower,
Happiness did you shower,
To the world, and into my heart.
Seemed ages, before your start.

Now two more roses and a bud,
Their feelings make you proud.
The first one ever, they look at.
You, like a hero they've just met!

The stories they would tell,
To Generations, before you fell.
Your beauty, fragrance, softness,
Sharing the same consciousness.

A simple story yes, oft repeated.
Not well understood or heeded.
This for every one that withers,
Know yourself deep, before others.

Chalat Rajaram 02122022 1:20PM

YOUR LOVE

You care for me, for my body and spirit.
You comfort my pain, bathe me, and turn me.
You help heal my open wounds,
The pain, physical and emotional.

You are a team, health aide, nurse.
Doctor, chaplain, social worker.
You keep coming into my home,
Trying to help my dying body.

You deal with my inadequacies.
My family for better or for worse.
For yours is not to judge, you give love.
Your combined kindness envelops me.

Now, I must leave, help me learn how to.
Medicate me, massage me, and give me your gentle touch.
I came to this earth with love,
I am blessed now to leave with your love.

Chalat Rajaram 2:20PM 4/19/11

Chapter 5

AMERICAN JOURNEYS

ALASKA

Where you mightily rose from,
Your expansive oceans, miles of river.
Dressed up sometimes, as at a prom,
Changing intricate patterns, nature's weaver.

Never imagined how far and remote,
Stories of rock, iceberg, moss, and silt.
Access to some parts by air, ship, or boat,
Land on rising rock, how your forests were built.

Thundering sounds of crashing glacier,
Calves in the ocean, floating iceberg melts.
Sounds of seagull, seal, blowing whale, to hear.
Alaska, of wondrous beauty, memories so dear.

Chalat Rajaram 07122014

ALASKAN MEMORIES

The changing skies, shifting clouds on the horizon.
Cold winds, shining northward the sun.
Going through seas, straits, more sailing to be done.
Glaciers, the salmon on their yearly run.

Pictures, videos to take, shows to see.
Foods to explore and taste, spirits and ale.
People to meet, FIFA world cup at sea!
Books to read, poems to write, no worry about mail.

Bald eagles, their huge nests, growing baby birds.
Sea otter, seals, and humpback whales.
The raven held high, in rank of the wizards.
The salmon run each year that never fails.

The hike after leaving ship, up and higher to Dewey Lake.
At Skagway, memories of the old gold rush place.
Sitting by the water, the words now take shape.
Of Alaskan memories, I write at my pace.

Chalat Rajaram 07172014 1:30PM

ANCHORAGE

Now as the plane readies to fly,
I ponder as I glance over your sky.
Looking down from oh so high,
My heart does not question why?

Hearty people, striving, always smiling.
Putting up with the weather, so daunting.
Modern rugged, see the moose crossing!
Long evenings, bright, the sun still shining.

Anchorage, from air, water, rail, and land.
Applause, with many a clapping hand.
Thank you for lifting and soothing my heart,
Cleansing my spirit here, as we depart.

Chalat Rajaram 07172014 11AM

CHICAGO SKY

Blue endless clear sky,
Red hues of distant setting sun.
As I look down from up high,
Sheets of white, the land adorns.

Shining now everywhere, many a golden light.
My eyes catch shapes forming many a jewel.
Their reflections this night on the large lake,
Suddenly, the sky dark like a black well.

Chicago, of large expansive land.
Of glorious sky and large water.
Deep under the snow, your gritty sand.
Your open heart, windy howling laughter.

Chalat Rajaram 03062010

CLOUDS OVER OHIO

As the plane climbs over the clouds,
So many more in the far distance.
Large white, very tall ones like snow cones.
Rain bearing dark clouds, interspersed.

Like tears from so many eyes,
Celebration of a birth, grief over death.
Life with the beginning and end,
Changes with suffering over poor health.

Within the clouds now, mixed emotions.
Prayers seeking many connections.
Rain turns to a sudden thunderstorm.
Different energy fields around, collide.

Night falls over Ohio, the clouds engulf.
Written words are liberating.
Optimism, enthusiasm, hope.
As the plane lowers to land.

Chalat Rajaram 07112006

DEVI AT TUSTIN

Devi at Attukal Bhagavathi Temple,
Manifested as an elderly woman.
A smile from ear to ear,
Guiding my entry into
The top of the snaking line.
She was here today too,
At Tustin, an elderly Caucasian.
Sitting at the driver's seat.
Bags of clothing arranged,
Around her minivan, beckoning.
Can you carry these to my porch?
Mumbling about my back unheard,
No further questions, I helped.
Remembering the words from afar.
"Am I not the mother to all?"
Still ringing in my ear, as I
Continued the walk, after
Seeing Devi at Tustin suddenly today.

Chalat Rajaram 01232023 6:45PM

DOHENY STATE BEACH

A strip of the ocean,
At Doheny State Beach.
The waves crash on the shores,
As gulls and Pelicans, hover.
Balancing in the wind,
The Sunbeams spread over them.
The same sun, ocean, and sand,
Attracts people of all ages.
All day and evening to walk,
To run, to pedal, sit and gaze.
The thoughts and vision,
Entering deeper, into the hearts
Of all. The same Consciousness.
The happiness in all, felt and seen.
The water, ocean, trees, birds, fish.
Sharing the One. Unfiltered, same.
This strip of beach in my view.
Doheny state beach. Always.
Unchanging. Peace. Love.

Chalat Rajaram 02072022 9:17AM

FLYING TO LADY LOVE

This long stop at Phoenix,
Has got my mind in a fix!
It's crazy waiting on this plane,
Watching outside, the falling rain.
Composing poems near the midnight hour,
Seeing Austin through dent in the cloud.
Thinking sleepily about my dreaming flower,
As I start counting the minutes aloud.
Destiny has brought us together,
Together to face every change of weather.
I feel lighthearted like a dove,
As I think of happy days, my love.
Phoenix, Austin, I fly above.
To come to the lady, I love.
Your love, will I treasure.

Chalat Rajaram 03281985

FOR THE GARDENERS AT ACACIA

If you are a gardener in Orange County,
Be thankful for the sun, watch out for the bee!

If you love roses, and they in turn love you!
Feed them food 'n water, they'll bloom all year too!

If you love the dirt, weeds, leaves and root,
Growing vegetables and fruit, it's a hoot!!

So dear friends and gardeners, enjoy your toil,
While I you a poem write, have fun in the soil!!

GLACIER THOUGHTS

Compressed ice over thousand years,
Ice fields under clouds, hundreds of miles.
Mostly receding, little advance, large glaciers.
Thunderous calving, ice on piles.

Icebergs float for miles around,
Even where the fish abound.
Migratory birds, seagulls, seek fish.
The seals feast on quite a dish.

Mendenhall, Hubbard, many a glacier name.
Sustaining Alaskan life for another thousand years.
Receding, new forests form. Never the same!
Moss over rock, dead trees. Stories one never hears.

Chalat Rajaram 07172014 2PM

MINNEAPOLIS BURNING

Knee on neck as life leaves,
Pleading, yet the cry unheard.
Striking at the core of beliefs,
Of human dignity lost, as feared.

Too slow to call out injustice.
People taking to the street.
At such moment this pandemic,
The stopping of a heartbeat.

Plea in Navajo, Spanish, English.
Tears and grief, this gnawing deep.
Wherefore we headed, is there a wish?
Is there a soul, why can't we weep?

The launch of dragon rocket today,
Brings pride and joyful celebration.
US-built and launched this end of May.
A smile amidst this deep depression.

Over hundred thousand dead this year,
The country is reeling, far from healing.
Impatience bursting, hard to bear.
As Minnesota, Minneapolis is burning.

Chalat Rajaram 05302020 12:45PM

MY HEART IS IN ALASKA

Through Ketchikan, Juneau, Skagway.
Whittier, Anchorage, Denali, Glacier Bay.
Wide eyed and ready, you came to me.
At every place, different sights to see.

Gorgeous mountains, forests of trees.
Roaring rivers and rapids, flights of geese.
Wilderness, to see, feel your cold breeze.
Summer is ending, the lakes will soon freeze.

Call of the wild, lynx, big bear.
Big horned Dall sheep, the wolf to fear.
Running salmon, climbing ladders in river.
Rainy days wet and cold, many a shiver.

My heart is in Alaska.
Now to fly away so far.
Let your spirit linger for long,
As the sweet words of a song.

Chalat Rajaram 07172014 12 Noon

PACIFIC OCEAN

The streak of the sun,
Lining the Pacific Ocean.
Men, women, and children,
At the Pacific coast and the Caribbean.
At nights, lights from cities and oil drills,
Golf courses, trees blowing in the breeze.
Rain drops soon fall on the head,
Get back in, watch the ocean from my bed.

Chalat Rajaram 03222017

SNOWMASS WONDER

Rafting down the rapids at Shoshone River,
Examining the lodges of the resident beaver.
Breathing the thin air, feeling the whizzing wind.
Biking down Maroon Bells to Aspen, feeling the grind.
Climbing high on gondolas and lift chairs,
Hiking up and down Snowmass, Aspen, without fear.
Riding on the sturdy, beautiful horses,
Along the mountain trails, in twos and fours.
Driving, walking, biking, listening, watching.
Taking in the splendor and beauty, then writing.
Colorado, Aspen, Snowmass!
Your beauty is difficult to surpass.

Chalat Rajaram 08211999

SUNSET OVER VEGAS

As the golden sun sets,
Sinking behind the tall rocky hills.
The city that never rests,
Bathed in the glow, add the frills.

Memories in everyone.
Visitors, family, and friend.
This place is not one and done,
Invokes emotions hard to blend.

Vegas bright lights and setting sun,
Sin city, attracting child, woman, man.
Beautiful, to have good times and fun,
Love it or hate it, either you are, or not a fan!

Chalat Rajaram (Phoenix) 6/16/16 9:20AM

THE DESERT

The desert heated by the midday sun,
Somewhere the sound of the rattlesnake.
The lizard darting, the click of the gun.
Beware, because this cowboy's no fake.

His scarred face, hat slouched over face.
Unaware of the fly perched on his nose.
Spurs on his boots, the distant haze.
Words from his mouth is no prose.

The gunslinger remains unaware,
As the bounty hunter approaches.
Let's leave the end open, bare
Note the gun went off, it's your guess!

Chalat Rajaram 02122017

THOUGHTS FLYING HIGH

Thinking at twenty-five thousand feet,
Where time and space, thoughts meet.
At the speed the plane flies,
The mind very soon tires.
Concentration begins to waver,
Sleep trying to soon take over.
In my tired head, I hear voices.
Of the plane's engines; other noises.
Drowning out the thoughts flying high,
As El Paso lights appear through the night sky.

Chalat Rajaram 03311985 10:20PM

THOUGHTS THROUGH INDIO

Thought of you, as I passed Indio.
Used to tease you whenever we did.
In your sleep then and now,
Sweet memories, as past Gila Bend I speed.

Phoenix has changed long after Tolleson,
You would not recognize the many
Changes, architecture, construction.
Our talks, memories, some zany.

Phoenix, and then off to Tucson.
We spoke of our trip here long ago.
Your good heart that loved fun now gone,
Time holds changes, that none know.

The windmills turn near Palm Springs,
The cacti grow tall and old.
The red rock and the creek the water brings,
Your love and kindness always shone like gold.

Chalat Rajaram 01312017

TRAIL ABOVE SKAGWAY

As I try to empty my mind,
Undo thoughts, help me unwind.
Here, hundreds of feet above the bay.
Rugged trek on the trail above Skagway.

Lake Dewey, tranquil, quite lazy.
Rain drops over me, the sky appears hazy.
My mind feels peaceful, oh so tranquil!
The water is so expansive, beautiful, and still.

Alaska, of mighty mountain and glacier.
Big whale, bald eagle, bear, and deer.
Harsh weather, rain, snow, and sleet.
Drawing me close, your beauty is no easy feat!

Chalat Rajaram 07122014

TURBULENCE

It's 8:30 and I am a bit late,
EMTs on the 405, got to stop and wait.
133 the alternate route to the 5, it's almost 9!
Twenty past 10, the doors shut on my plane.

Exit Jamboree, now speeding across.
To 405 again, exit MacArthur, no pause.
To Main Street parking, then the wait again.
The shuttle driver sits, looks, and finally drives to my lane.

Jovial and kind, no hurry for this fellow.
Imagining all that could have gone wrong, I say hello!
Dropping me at the airline departures, it's now 9:30
Baggage check-in, long frisk down by TSA security.

Walking in towards the gate, the boarding lines are long.
Chicago, here I come! Feel like bursting into a song!
Managing stress, trusting the self, mindfulness.
Amidst the turbulence, a stream of brightness.

Chalat Rajaram 03082016 11:30AM

UVA GRADUATION

Sinking into the clouds again,
The CRJ 700 bobs a bit side to side.
Climbing over Chicago in the rain,
Richmond now looks green and wide.

Beautiful blue skies I see afar,
The sun brightens the flaky clouds.
Thoughts of road below the rental car,
I ponder driving over hill and mounds.

Charlottesville and the university,
My nephew, his coming graduation.
Excited to be here in a new city,
The plane lands at final destination.

Returning from Richmond to Houston,
From grayer skies the night so brawn.
Westward sky clouds now lighter,
As the EMB 145 hugs them tighter.

Memories come at me of days past,
Visits to NASA, screeching parakeets.
Of friends and home cooked food,
Bring them back again, if only I could.

Now, off to Santa Ana and John Wayne,
Time to settle down, forget the pain.
To sit back, close my eyes and pray.
Today, many a relevance, it's 21st May.

Chalat Rajaram 5/19/17 4:22PM modified on 5/21/17

MEMORIES OF WIND

Getting out this morning,
The sun, warm and benevolent.
The Santa Ana's kicking up,
Swirls, and full-on pressure.
The camera, picking up
Motion of the trees, swaying.
Birds chattering in the branches.
A few are caught up on irregular flights,
Some sit on rooftops, just sunbathing.
Memories of walks long ago, on such days,
Windswept amongst paddy fields.
The wind chimes speaking,
The same words of the mighty wind.
Memories of temple bells in a
Faraway land, same awareness always.
A small insect crossing the road,
Feeling windy vibrations on the cement below.
The warmth, the wind, the One.

Chalat Rajaram 03072022 10:17AM

Printed in the United States
by Baker & Taylor Publisher Services